Watson's Notes

SPECTRUM +

I. KALISKY & D. KEDEM

UNIT 2
Exploring Basic

APRIL 1985

All programs in this book have been written expressly to illustrate specific teaching points. They are not warranted as being suitable for any particular application. Every care has been taken in the writing and presentation of this book but no responsibility is assumed by the author or publishers for any errors or omissions contained herein.

ISBN 0 907792 57 X

Published by:

Glentop Publishers Ltd
Standfast House
Bath Place
High Street
Barnet
Herts EN5 1ED
Tel: 01–441–4130

TABLE OF CONTENTS

FOREWORD

BEGINNING WITH COLOUR AND SOUND.....

We shall begin this second teaching unit by talking about colour and sound.

To start, enter the following short program into the computer, don't worry if you don't understand it all at this stage. Remember, to hold down CAPS SHIFT to get capital letters like 'N'.

```
10 FOR N=1 TO 6
20 BORDER N
30 PAPER 7-N : CLS
40 BEEP 0.2, 2 * N
50 NEXT N
60 GO 10
```

Run the program.

What is happening here? How are the colour and sound operations created.

The secret lies in the two lines:

```
10 FOR N=1 TO 6
. . .
. . .
. . .
50 NEXT N
```

In this teaching unit we shall 'crack the code', so that you fully understand these commands. We'll see that they open up a whole world of possibilities for us: everything from constructing a digital clock, to drawing pyramids and interesting geometric shapes. It's worth knowing that these new commands are some of the most commonly used in BASIC.

Stop the program and display it on the screen.

If you can't see the program change the paper colour:

```
PAPER 0
```

and then press ENTER twice.

Now go on and study Chapter 1, but don't erase the program from the memory yet.

Chapter 1

VARIABLES

☐ Look at the program that you've just put into the computer. You'll see that in nearly every line the letter N appears. What is the function of this 'mysterious' N? In this chapter we're going to solve the mystery!

☐ First erase the program from the computer's memory. (Can't remember how – turn to Unit 1)

And now...

☐ Type in the following program:

```
10 LET N=1
20 PRINT AT 10,15;N
```

❓ When you run the program __/__ (1, 10) appears on the screen?

❓ What will happen if we change line 10 to:

```
10 LET N=2
```

(If you're not sure check it on the computer for yourself and when you've tried it return line 10 to the way it was before.)

Now, we'll look at the two commands and explain exactly what they do:

Line 10: in this line the computer is told:

☐ LET N be equal to : __/__ (1,3)

When the computer has carried this out it remembers that N is equal to 1.
It then goes on to carry out line 2Ø.

Line 2Ø: in this line the computer is told:

PRINT AT position 1Ø,15 the VALUE of N, which in this case is equal to __/__ .

? What will be printed, if in line 2Ø you put inverted commas around N,i.e. "N" ?

```
2Ø PRINT AT 1Ø,15;"N"
```

☐ Make the change in the program and run it.

? Let's see what happens when N appears between inverted commas ("N"). The computer understands it as a __L__ (letter, number)?

? When N appears without inverted commas (N) the computer understands it as a __N__ (letter, number)?

? What will the following program do:

```
1Ø LET N=1
2Ø PRINT AT 1Ø,15;"N=";N
```

? On the screen you'll see: __N 1__ ?

☐ Change the line and check the answer.

? What will happen if you add to the program the following two lines:

```
3Ø LET N=2
4Ø PRINT AT 1Ø,15;"N=";N
```

☐ When you've thought about it, add the lines and run the new program.

The SPECTRUM+ is a fast-thinking computer and it will carry out the program very quickly. To follow what's happening insert, between lines 2Ø and 3Ø, the command PAUSE, e.g.

```
25 PAUSE 2Ø
```

After you've added the pause, run the program.

⬜Now add two more lines so that the program will write on the screen:

First: N=1
then: N=2
and then: N=3

    5Ø _____
    6Ø _____

Don't forget to put a pause between lines 4Ø and 5Ø.

Now you're going to write a program that will count many many more numbers....

Wait! Don't start to write the program yet!

It's important to know that you don't need to work hard and write a lot of commands, all you need to do is write a five line program:

```
1Ø LET N=1
2Ø PRINT AT 1Ø,15;"N=";N
25 PAUSE 2Ø
3Ø LET N=N+1
4Ø GO TO 2Ø
```

⬜Add lines 3Ø and 4Ø. (By the way, notice how the new lines, 3Ø and 4Ø, replace the old lines 3Ø and 4Ø and erase them automatically!)

⬜You must erase lines 5Ø and 6Ø which aren't needed now. (Can't remember how? – turn to Unit 1)

⬜When you've finished typing in the program above, run it.

Look at what's happening on the screen: does this remind you of a digital clock. (A few pages further on, you're going to construct a clock of this kind).

❓ Why does the program count.... and count... and count? It's obvious that the reason why it goes on counting is to do with lines 3Ø and 4Ø, that you've added to the program.

Let's go through it step by step and see how the program works:

Line 1Ø: when the computer completed line 1Ø, N was equal to _1_ (1, 2, 3)?

Line 2Ø: When the computer completed line 2Ø, it printed: N = _N_ ?

Line 3Ø: In this line we're telling the computer: Let N be a new number which is equal to the previous number (1) plus 1:

$$3Ø \text{ LET N} = N + 1$$
$$\quad\quad\quad \uparrow \quad\quad \uparrow$$
$$\quad\quad\quad \text{new} \quad \text{previous}$$

(In our case: N =1 + 1)

When the computer has completed line 3Ø, it **erases from its memory** the previous value of N, which was: _1_ (1, 2)?

Now it remembers that the new value of N is: ____ (1, 2)? In its memory the computer knows that now N = _2_ ?

Line 4Ø: we already know the command GO TO from Unit 1. This tells the computer to go back and repeat line _2Ø_ in our program?

Let's study the way N changes as the computer carries out the program. Imagine for a moment, that you are the computer. Go through line by line and write, in the spaces below, the value of N in each line:

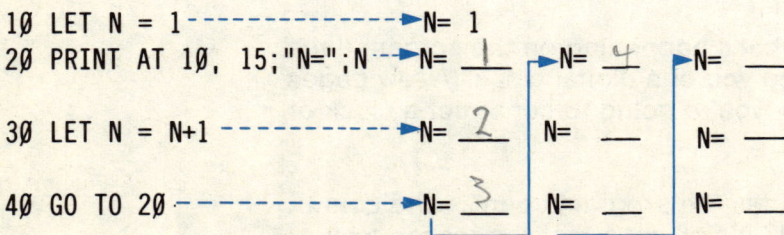

```
1Ø LET N = 1 - - - - - - - - - - - - ▶ N= 1
2Ø PRINT AT 1Ø, 15;"N=";N - - ▶ N= _1_    ▶N= _4_    ▶N= ___

3Ø LET N = N+1 - - - - - - - - - ▶ N= _2_    N= ___    N= ___

4Ø GO TO 2Ø - - - - - - - - - - - ▶ N= _3_    N= ___    N= ___
```

(Do you find this difficult? Look at Answer 14)

NOTE

Because N changes its value every time the computer moves on, it is called a VARIABLE.

Remember! The computer keeps in its memory only the last number that the variable was equal to. The computer doesn't keep several values for the same variable, only one!

Look at the screen again. You'll see the computer is still counting and counting very patiently. If you don't stop it, will it carry on to infinity?

The computer can count up to the gigantic number 10'38 (one with a "tail" of 38 zeros, and it will take it many years to get there).

Stop the program running.

(Can't remember how? – see Unit 1)

Erase the whole program from the computer's memory. Now, while the computer's memory is clear, it's time for a game...

GAMES CORNER: 'RACE TO 500'

Using the commands that you've learnt so far you can play a little game by yourself or with your friends.

Type in the following program:

```
10 LET N=1
20 PRINT AT 10, 10 ; "START"
30 LET N=N+1
40 GO TO 30
```

There isn't a key for 'START' on the computer.
Type in the word letter by letter.

Run the program.

? Is the computer counting on the screen
____ (yes,no)?

But, remember that the computer is counting all the time! (All the time the computer is going from line 30 to 40 and back again...)

Do you want proof that it is counting?

⬜ First stop the program running (BREAK).

Then, to find out which number it has got to, type:

    PRINT N

and don't forget to finish with ENTER.

? Look at the screen. Which number has it got to ____ ?

(This number is the value of N at the moment that the program was stopped.)

⬜ Go back and run the program again from the beginning.

⬜ Stop the computer and check which number it has got to.

Now for the game: 'RACE TO 500':

Object of the game: to stop the computer running when it gets to 500 or as close as possible.

How to play: each player in turn gets five tries. With each try, run the program, and stop it (by pressing BREAK) when you think the computer has counted up to 500.

Every player must remember the closest that they've got to 500. (PRINT N and then ENTER). The one who gets number closest to 500 is the winner!

If you have finished playing, we'll move on......

ERRORS IN A PROGRAM

We have to write a program which will print consecutive even numbers in the centre of screen (2, 4, 6 ...).

In order to do this, an experienced programmer wrote the following program:

```
10 LET N=2
20 PRINT AT 10, 15 ; N
25 PAUSE 20
30 LET N = N+1
40 GO TO 20
```

⬜ Copy the program as it is and RUN it.

❓ Does the program carry out the task (it has to print 2, 4, 6 ... in the centre of the screen)?

The Program has a BUG – an error.

You typed in the program properly but it does not do what you wanted. What happened? Even professional programmers do not write programs in 'one go'. After they have written and run the program they often discover all sorts of errors which are known as 'BUGS'. They do not give up! They sit and think until they find the bug and then rectify it.

You also have to patient. If you have finished writing a program, or part of it, run it. If you discover that it does not carry out what you wanted, find the bugs!

⬜ Now, find the bug in the program above.

❓ If you have found the Bug enter the corrections in the program and run it. Did you overcome the Bug?

(Having difficulties? Turn to Answer 2.)

❓ What do you have to do to the program so that odd numbers will appear consecutively in the centre of the screen (1, 3, 5 ...)?

? What, in your opinion, will the following program do?

```
10 LET X=5
20 PRINT X
25 PAUSE 20
30 LET X = X+5
40 GO TO 20
```

▢ Check your answer on the computer. Notice that we called our variable X this time, instead of N as in previous programs.

RULE: Names of variables must start with a letter after which we can add more characters, either letters and figures.

Here are a few examples of names of variables: X1, N1K, AB1, XY, Z.

▢ What will happen if you type the following line into the computer:

```
20 LET 1X=2
```

▢ Type this line in and run the program.

? What does the computer tell you? Did the question mark appear?

This signifies that there is a 'spelling mistake' in the program.

The computer tells you that there is a 'syntax error' in the line. The reason is that it is not permitted to have a number as the first character of a variables.

▢ Change the name of the variable to X1. Does the computer accept the line now?

Computer Message '2'

? What will the following program do:

```
20 PRINT AT 10, 15; Z
25 PAUSE 20
30 LET Z = Z + 100
40 GO TO 20
```

⬛ Type it in and run it.

❓ What did the computer tell you?

At the bottom of the screen message number 2 appears:

```
2 variable not found, 20 : 1
```

The computer is telling you that there is a variable, in the first command in line 20 (20 : 1), the name of which it does not know. Therefore it cannot carry out the command.

❓ The name of the variable is ____ ?
The computer does not know what number to print at position 10, 15.

REMEMBER! The variable must have a value.

(If you still do not understand, we shall try another direction. Pretend you are a computer, if you had to carry out line 20 and print the value of Z, could you do it without knowing its value?)

⬛ Add a line which you will give the variable an initial value and run the program.

⬛ Remove the program from the computer's memory and continue..

A. Write a program which will draw the following pattern (for this exercise call your variable M.)

If you do not remember how to get out of the SCROLL turn to Unit 1

(Answer 3).

B. Now improve the program so that commas will appear between the numbers,e.g. 1, 2, 3, 4 .....

Do you need help?

(Do not forget inverted the commas and use semi–colons.)

(If you still have problems, turn to Answer 4)

C. The computer works very quickly and fills the screen with numbers. We shall now ask you to enter a suitable line in the program so that the computer will fill the screen at a slower rate **without** using the PAUSE command.

(If you do not know what to do you can get a hint in Unit 1).

After you have tried, you can compare your effort with Answer 5.

By now you should know that the second number in the BEEP command gives the pitch level. Let's check what pitch we can reach. We shall use the program from the previous exercise for this.

Use the variable M within the BEEP command in order to find the highest level of pitch it is possible to reach.

(Hint: you saw that the higher the pitch the greater the second number in the BEEP command. Try and think where to put the variable M in order to check which level of pitch it reaches).

(Answer 6)

Computer Message 'B'

When you ran the program it stopped when the variable M reached 70 and the following message appeared:

```
B INTEGER OUT OF RANGE, 25 : 1
```

The pitch level can only go up to 69. As M reached 7Ø the computer produce a very high BEEP and announced that, in line 25 in the first command (25 : 1), there is a BEEP which it cannot perform.

Are you having difficulties? Turn to the next hint.

Hint: Look at the following two lines:

```
1Ø LET Y = 1
2Ø PRINT AT Y, 11; "A"
```

What do these lines do?

Copy and run them.

◻ Now add two more lines so that all the A's are printed.

(Answer 8)

Computer Message '5

Our variable in the print command increased to reach a value which was off the screen:

    PRINT AT 22,11

Therefore the computer informs us ' 5 OUT OF SCREEN '.

Meaning, the computer was told to print outside the screen area.

☐ Now alter line 20 so that these numbers appear instead of the A's: 1, 4, 7, 10, 13....

(Answer 9)

☐ Now change the program so that instead of the numbers, coloured squares will appear in the 7 colours from black (0) to Yellow (6). (Hint: You have to define another variable as well as using the INK command in order to colour the squares.)

(Answer 10)

☐ Now add a BEEP command as well, using the variable of the colour in order to give a note with rising pitch.

(Hint: In order to achieve a big difference in the pitch of the notes, you can multiply the variable by 3 for example.)

(Answer 11)

☐ Delete the program from the computer's memory.

THE 'TIRED' PROGRAM

❓ Can you guess what the following program does?

```
10 LET X=1
20 PRINT X; "," ;
30 PAUSE X*X
40 LET X=X+1
50 GO TO 20
```

Why did we call it the 'tired' program?
Run the program and check for yourself.

(If you do not understand turn to Answer 12.)

AND IN CONCLUSION .....

What will the following program do?

```
10 LET M=0
20 PRINT AT M, M; "█"
30 LET M=M+1
40 GO TO 20
```

Think carefully before you type in and run the program.

After you have decided what will happen, run the program and see if you were right.

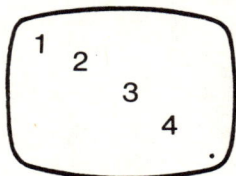

Did the program do what you thought it would do?

(If not, turn to Answer 13.)

Now the time has come to play with the computer on your own. Draw all sorts of vertical, horizontal and diagonal lines with various characters, colours and notes.

Chapter 2

LOOPS

Now that you have become familiar with the idea of variables, we can turn to understanding the following lines

```
10 FOR N=1 TO 6
 . . .
 . . .
 . . .
50 NEXT N
```

These lines appeared in the changing colours program at the beginning of the Unit.

Type in and run the following program.

```
10 FOR N=1 TO 50
20 PRINT AT 10, 15; N: BEEP 0, 2,N
30 NEXT N
40 PRINT "END"
```

Do you already understand how the FOR...NEXT commands work?

To help you, let's follow the program line by line:

LINE 10:Here the computer is told to let the variable N start as 1 (FOR N=1) and to continue until it is 50 (TO 50).

LINE 20:Here the computer carrys out two commands. First it prints, at position 10, 15, the value of N. Second, it plays the sound at pitch N.

LINE 30:Here the computer is told to increase N by 1 and return to line 10. However if N has already passed 50 and reached 51, **do not** return to line 10 t go on to line 40.

Check for yourself, to see if you have understood. Imagine you are the computer and write the values of N in the empty spaces:

```
10 FOR N=1 TO 3------►N= ___  ► N= ___  ►N= ___  ► N= ___

20 PRINT AT 10,15;N--►N= ___   N= ___    N= ___    N= ___

30 NEXT N -----------► N= ___   N= ___    N= ___    N= ___

40 PRINT "END"        N= ___    N= ___    N= ___    N= ___
```

"END"?   "END"?   "END"?   "END"?

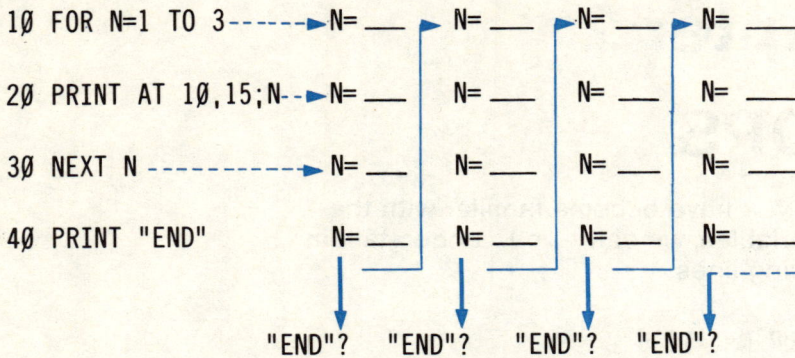

Decide when you print "END" too.

(Answer 14)

Let's return to the program in the computer.

What will happen if we change the 50 to 60 in line 10?

Change line 10 to:

    10 FOR N=1 TO 60

and run the program.

This time the program counts to ____ ?

What will happen if we change N=1 to N=5 at 10 like this:

    10 FOR N=5 TO 60

The program will count from ____ to ____?

Try it and see if you were right.

What will happen if you erase line 30 completely?

Erase line 30 and run the program.

The only number the computer printed was: ____ (5, 10, 20, 30)?

You can see that without line 30 the computer will not return to line 10. It only prints the first value of N (in this case 5) and stopped.

Consider the following two programs:

```
PROGRAM A              PROGRAM B

10 FOR X=1 TO 50       10 LET X=1
20 PRINT AT 10, 15; X  20 PRINT AT
                          10, 15; X
30 NEXT X              30 LET X=X+1
                       40 GO TO 20
```

There are loops in both programs. A loop is a part of a program that the computer goes round and carries out again and again.

☐ In program A the loop is produced by the FOR...NEXT loop. In program B the loop is produced by GO TO.

Consider the following program:

```
10 PRINT "START"
20 FOR N=1 TO 200
30 NEXT N
40 PRINT "END"
```

❔ What does this program do?

❔ What are the functions of lines 20 and 30?

They replace a command you know. What is the command. When you have thought about it ....

☐ Type in and run the program.

❔ Now do you know which command they replace?

❔ What should you do to increase the time between the appearance of START and the appearance of END?

☐ Check your assumption on the computer!

The pair of lines 20 and 30 in the program caused a delay and, in fact, replaced the PAUSE command.

⬜ When the computer reaches lines 20 and 30, it runs round between the _____ (20, 30, 100, 200) times and when it finishes it goes on to line 40.

The time in which the computer carried out the 200 'cycles' in the loop, creates the delay. So, the larger the number of cycles between the two lines (the loop), the longer the delay we get.

⬜ Change line 20 so that you get a delay twice as long.

⬜ Create a program which will do the following:

● colour the border in all the colours from black to white (0 to 7).

● with the pitch of the sound rising.

● the colours having finished, the computer begins again.

(Answer 15)

⬜ Now add another line to the program, so that the computer will colour the screen using numbers descending from 7 to 0 while the colour of the border rises from 0 to 7.

(Answer 16)

Now, compare the program you have developed with the program that appeared on page 5 . Did you manage to "work" it out?

WHAT HAVE YOU LEARNED UP 'TIL NOW?

In this Unit you have learned two very important concepts!
  1. You became acquainted with variables.
  2. You learned to recognise a loop produced by using the commands FOR...NEXT.

In the rest of the unit, we will make additional use of the concepts we have learned.

HERE ARE A FEW IDEAS TO CONCLUDE THE CHAPTER

A. Write a program to draw seven A's diagonally across the centre of the screen. (Use FOR...NEXT).

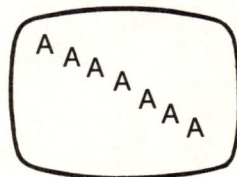

_____
_____
_____

(Hint: Consider the program on page 19)

(Answer 17)

B. Add other lines to the program so that the computer will print another 7 A's going diagonally in the other direction like this:

(from top to bottom).

_____
_____
_____
_____

(Hint: Reduce the number of the column each time by 1, e.g. LET X=X=-1)

(Answer 18)

⬜Write a program to place your name on the screen 5 times like this:

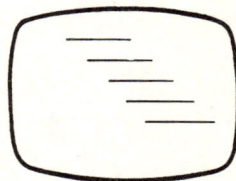

_____
_____
_____
_____

(Again, use FOR...NEXT)

(Answer 19)

Chapter 3

CONSTRUCTING A DIGITAL CLOCK

Now that you understand the FOR...NEXT commands, you can construct a digital clock using the computer. If you have a digital clock at home it is advisable to have it by your side while you are designing the clock on the computer.

Counting the Seconds

First let's concentrate on displaying the seconds on the clock.

Think about the numbers showing the seconds on a digital clock. Then answer:
    The clock starts counting the seconds from ____ (∅, 1)?

Does the number 6∅ appear ____ (yes, no)?

You can see that a digital clock starts from ∅, reaches 59 and then, instead of showing 6∅, goes back to ∅ and starts again.

In order to do the same thing on the computer, let's construct the program in stages:

A. For the first stage, write a program to count from ∅ – 59 in the middle of the screen.

Include a PAUSE command too, in order to slow down the rate at which the numbers change.

Run the program.

(Answer 2∅)

B. For the second stage, add a command telling the computer to start again from Ø when it reaches 59.

——————————————————— (Answer 21)

⬜ Run the program.

C. There is a bug (a small problem) in your program. Can you see what it is?

(Answer 22)

D. Add a line to correct this.

———————————————

❓ Has the bug disappeared?

Hint: Remember how you erased the hands of to Robot in Unit 1.

(Answer 23)

Adjusting the Clock to Show Actual Seconds

❓ Is the rate that the numbers appear on the screen ——— (quicker, slower) than that of a real clock?

❓ How can you control the rate at which the numbers change on the screen, so as to match the rate of the clock?

❓ What PAUSE command should you enter into the program for the computer to count at the same rate as your clock (or as near as possible)?

PAUSE   ?

⬜ Carry out a few experiments until you reach the nearest rate to that of the seconds on the real clock.

(Answer 24)

Now Let's Count the Minutes

Consider a digital clock again. What happens when the digital clock, finishes counting a minute? Obviously enough, the minutes number increases by 1.

☐ You should add a suitable command to the program so that the clock counts minutes too.

(Hint: add a suitable FOR...NEXT loop to the program).

☐ Be sure that your program carries out the following things:

The screen should look like this:

$$Ø \; : \; Ø$$

minutes   seconds

The colon (:) separating the minutes from the seconds never changes position.

☐ Remember the bug we had when counting the seconds? (The 9 was not erased.) Take care that the bug does not return when counting the minutes.

(Answer 25)

Let's stop for a minute and consider our program. There are two FOR...NEXT loops in it:

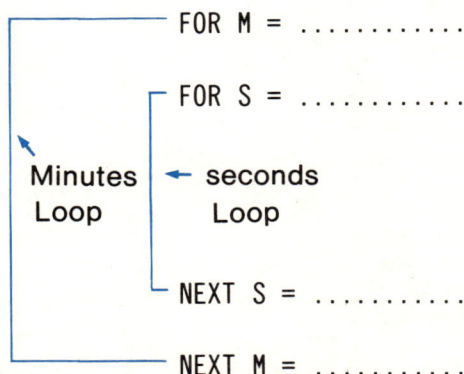

```
        FOR M = . . . . . . . . . . .

          FOR S = . . . . . . . . . . .

Minutes ← seconds
Loop       Loop

          NEXT S = . . . . . . . . . .

        NEXT M = . . . . . . . . . .
```

We see that a number of FOR...NEXT loops, 'nested' inside one another, can be used in a program.

❓ Is the computer capable of carrying out a program in which there are FOR…NEXT loops intersecting like this?

```
┌── FOR  K = ..........
│ ┌─ FOR  N = ..........
│ └─ NEXT K = ..........
└── NEXT N = ..........
```

(Answer 26)

❓ If you are not fed up with the clock yet, add hours to it (and the date ? ? ?)!

TO CONCLUDE

Add colours and sounds to your clock giving free reign to your imagination. (Our little idea is in Answer 27.)

Chapter 4

THE COMPUTER AS A DUPLICATION MACHINE

We'll start by duplicating simple graphics.

Here's a pound: £

The computer can duplicate lots of pounds for you. Using a FOR...NEXT loop write a program that will duplicate the pounds like this:

The £ key can be found here:

Do you need help?

Complete the following program:

```
1Ø FOR X= ___ TO
2Ø PRINT AT 4, ___ ; "£": PAUSE 1Ø
3Ø NEXT ___
```

Run the program.

⬜ Write a similar program that will duplicate the pounds thus:

```
   0  2  4  6  8 10 12 14 16 18 20 22 24 26 28 30
 0
 2
        £
 4      £
        £
 6      £
        £
 8      £
        £
10      £
        £
12      £
14
16
```

Now its up to you to write a program that will produce a 'pattern' of £s.

```
   0  2  4  6  8 10 12 14 16 18 20 22 24 26 28 30
 0
 2
         £ £ £ £ £ £ £ £ £
 4       £ £ £ £ £ £ £ £ £
         £ £ £ £ £ £ £ £ £
 6       £ £ £ £ £ £ £ £ £
         £ £ £ £ £ £ £ £ £
 8
10
12
14
16
```

❓ Having difficulty? Turn to the next page.

CLUE 1:

We want to write a program that will start to
print the top row of pounds, then move to the
next row and start from the beginning again,
continuing like that until it completes the
required number of rows.

The following diagram demonstrates how the
program print multiple pounds on the first 3
rows.

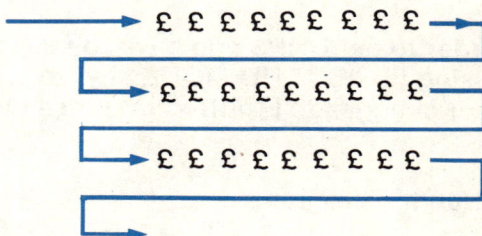

£ £ £ £ £ £ £ £ £

£ £ £ £ £ £ £ £ £

£ £ £ £ £ £ £ £ £

How do you write the program so that each
time it completes a row it automatically jumps
to the next row and again starts printing the
pounds?

If you can answer that question, you can
probably write the program.

Try now without using clue 2.

CLUE 2:

In the following program there are 2 lines to be
completed:

```
10 _____
20 FOR X = 5 TO 13
30 PRINT AT Y, X; "£"; PAUSE 10
40 NEXT X
50 _____
```

If you complete the lines correctly you will
have the required program.

(Answer 30)

Play around with the program and change the
size of the frame.

CHR$

☐ Now change line 3Ø to:

    3Ø PRINT AT Y, X; CHR$ 96; PAUSE 1Ø

The CHR$ key is here:

In order to get CHR$ you have to start by
pressing the EXTEND MODE key, so that the
cursor changes to ⊟ After that press the CHR$
key.

☐ Run the program.

？ What appeared on the screen? If you have
done things correctly you will again get a
screen full of pounds.

？ Why did this happen?

For every character, i.e. letter, number, graphic
and command on the keyboard there is a
specific code number permanently kept in the
computer's memory.

96 is the code number for the pound character
'£'.

CHR$ 96 tells the computer to get from its
memory the £ sign and therefore PRINT CHR$
96 tells the computer to print the '£'.

☐ Clear the screen and change the code to
CHR$ 37 and run the program.

In the manual that came with your
SPECTRUM+ there is a detailed list of all the
character codes.

☐ Open the book at the right page.

？ Which character has code number 33
___ (question mark, exclamation mark)?

You can see that the interesting characters start from code number 33.

Here's a challenge. Alter the program already in the computer so that it will draw a pattern of 7 lines across 15 columns.

We'll remind you what a row and column are.

● The computer starts printing with CHR$ 33.

● Each row will be a different colour (the top row Ø the bottom 7).

● The computer will print the characters in a different colour to the paper. (Because of this use the special command 'INK 9', that always gives the opposite colour to the paper.)

● Every time the pattern fills the screen, the computer should start again filling the pattern with additional characters, continuing until code 255.

☐ In the program use 3 FOR...NEXT loops 'nested inside one another.

Maybe you would also be interested in using beep or coloured squares.

☐ Try and write a program that will look like this:

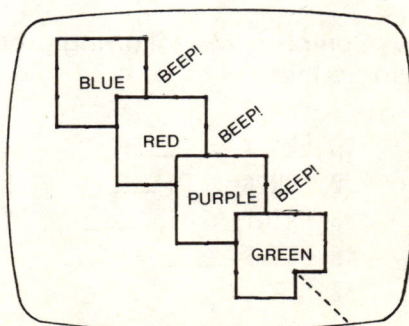

? Difficult? Work through to the following stages.

A. Write the program (using 2 FOR...NEXT loops) that will draw the first square (in the normal colour, black)

(Answer 31)

B. Enter (in the two FOR lines) variable A so that each time A grows it will print a square diagonally across the screen.

(Answer 32)

C. Add more lines to the program so that when A increases, after each square is drawn, you will get black squares diagonally across the screen as in the above picture.

(Answer 33)

D. Now enter another variable (on the PRINT line) so that each square is a different colour.

(Answer 34)

E. Finally after each square is drawn, the computer should make a sound that goes up or down from square to square.

(Answer 35)

USING STEP

We have to write a program that will duplicate 5 dollars:

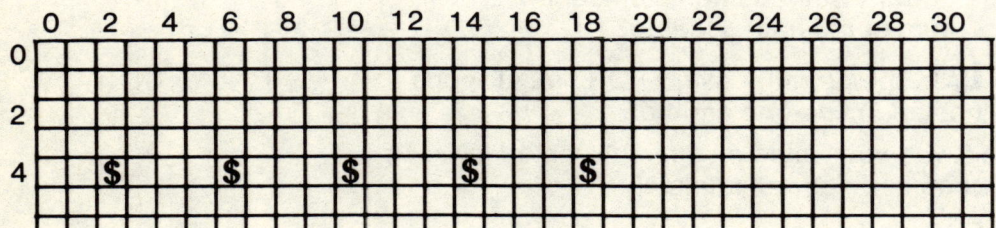

Complete the following program so that it can do that:

```
10 LET X = ____
20 FOR N=1 TO ____
30 PRINT AT 4, ____ ; "$"; PAUSE 10
40 LET X= ____ + ____
50 NEXT N
```

⬜ Enter the program into the computer and run it.

(Answer 36)

Completing the program:

We will shorten the program to only three lines! In order to do this you have to use the command:

STEP

⬜ Erase the existing program and enter the following:

```
10 FOR X=2 TO 18 STEP 4
20 PRINT AT 4 , X; "$"; PAUSE 10
30 NEXT X
```

⬜ Run the program.

❓ Did you get the same result as in the previous program?

❓ What do you think will happen if you change 'STEP 4' to 'STEP 2'?

⬜ Enter the change and see if you were right!

Let's summarise:

Adding STEP tells the computer to alter the variable in FOR...NEXT, in jumps' (STEPs) that match the number after STEP.

❓ STEP 4 tells the computer that the variable has to grow each time by ____?

❓ STEP 2 tells the computer that the variable increases each time by ____?

Add another two commands to the program so that it will print lines of $ spaced with 2 empty rows between each row like this:

(Answer 37)

What will the next program do?

```
10 FOR N=0 TO 40 STEP 5
20 PRINT N: PAUSE 10
30 NEXT N
```

After you have thought about it run it on the computer.

What, in your opinion, will happen in the next program?

```
10 FOR N=100 TO 0 STEP -10
20 PRINT N: PAUSE 10
30 NEXT N
```

Run it on the computer.

This time the computer 'went backwards', it started at 100 and arrived at 0.

Use a negative STEP in order to draw the diagonal lines shown on page 25. This time write the program so that it will draw the coloured square diagonally across.

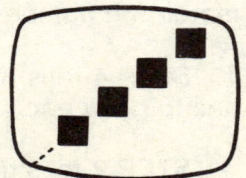

(Answer 38)

DUPLICATING ROBOTS

Now we will use the FOR...NEXT and STEP commands in order to duplicate shapes drawn on the screen.

Say hello to Roberta cousin of Robert from the previous unit:

⬜ Let's start writing the program that will draw Roberta.

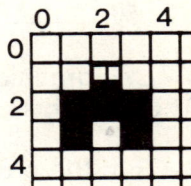

A. First enter the lines that will draw Roberta's head:

```
10 LET Y=1
20 LET X=2
30 PRINT PAPER 0 ; INK 9; AT Y,X; CHR$ 34
```

(Remember that INK 9 gives a white ink colour if the paper is dark and a black ink colour if the paper is light).

NOTE: in order to get the eyes we have used quotation marks code number 34, see Appendix 1.

We draw Roberta using the variables X and Y, so that we will be able to continue to duplicate her.

B. Now we have to add the shoulders and body.

⬜ The shoulders start one row _____ (above, below) the head, and one column _____ (left, right) of the head? Therefore the line to get the shoulders and body is:

```
40 PRINT AT Y + _____ ,X - _____ ; " ⬜⬜⬜ "
```

❓ Which numbers do you have to put in the empty spaces?

(Answer 39)

⬜ Now add the line and run it.

❓ Did you get the body in the right place?
(The body colour can be what you like.)

C. We will now do the legs.

(Answer 38)

⬜ Add a line that will draw the legs:

50 _____

⬜ Use graphics and space to get the legs.
(The colour is your choice.)

⬜ Run the program and check it.

(Answer 40)

D. Now let's duplicate Roberta on the screen:

You have add to and change the program so
that Roberta will appear 4 times across the
screen.

(Clue: use FOR...NEXT...STEP)

(Answer 41)

E. Now add the commands so that the
program will duplicate 3 rows of Roberta, one
underneath the other. (Think of how we got the
rows on page 36.)

(Answer 42)

F. Alter the program so that the robots appear
in different colours.

Finally:

● Duplicate Roberta on the diagonal.
● Duplicate her on both diagonals.

Chapter 5

ANIMATION: CREATING MOVEMENT ON THE SCREEN

Do you remember Robert doing morning exercises in the first unit? Now we will use the new skills you have acquired in order to move shapes on the screen.

EXERCISE 1

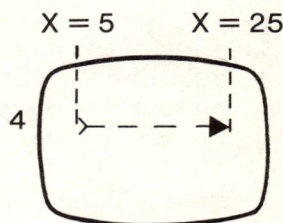

☐ Write a program that will move the character '>' across the screen, from column 5 to column 25, on row 4. When the > reaches the right edge it should start again, moving from left to right and so on. Ensure you know the commands you will need.

(If it is too hard for you, or you want to double check, turn to the hint on the next page)

Add colours and sounds as you wish.

HINT: Here is the program description:

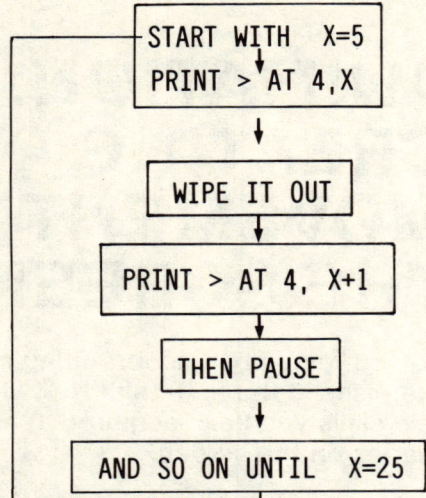

```
START WITH   X=5
PRINT > AT 4,X
        ↓
   WIPE IT OUT
        ↓
 PRINT > AT 4, X+1
        ↓
   THEN PAUSE
        ↓
 AND SO ON UNTIL   X=25
```

When it is finished return and start again.

⬜ Can you, from the above description, start
to write the program. Try, then run the program.
If you find any 'bugs' in the program, be patient
and try to fix them.

(Answer 43)

Comment: does the 'bird' fly too fast? Slow it
down with the help of PAUSE or BEEP.

EXERCISE 2

Alter the program so that in the beginning it
will show the > moving from left to right:
(coming out of 'wall' 1 and arriving at 'wall' 2).

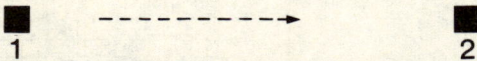

■ - - - - - - - - → ■
1   2

When the character arrives at wall 2, it should
turn around (into <) and move back to wall 1.

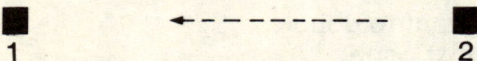

■ ← - - - - - - - - ■
1   2

When it reaches wall 1 it will turn round and so
on.

In writing the program ensure that:

● The bird (>) does not erase the 'walls'

● The bird continues to fly back and forth without stopping.

● The PAUSE or the BEEP occur between printing the bird and erasing it, and that they are suitably separated.

● The walls are not 'flickering'.

● When the bird is flying to the right the sound will rise and when it is flying to the left the sound descends.

● Each time the bird completes a circuit, the walls will change colour.

Compare the program you have written to that in Answer 44.

EXERCISE 3

Write a program that will draw 4 candles (as in the diagram). After the candles are lit the wind will appear (>) and move to the right extinguishing the candles:

Flame (multiplication sign)

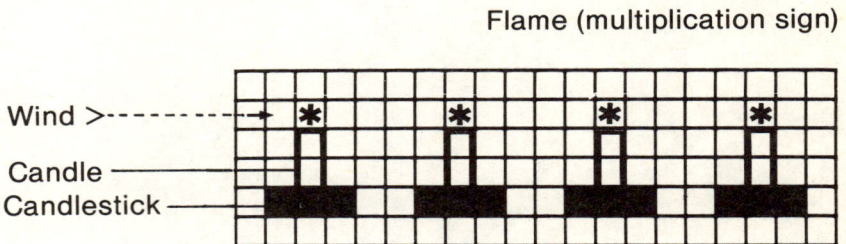

Wind >
Candle
Candlestick

Here are a few tips:

● The wind will move like the bird in the previous program.

● The flames are made from the multiplication sign *.

● Write the program to duplicate the candles the way we did with Roberta in the previous chapter. Put colours and sound in the program.

After persevering yourself you can turn and
compare your results with Answer 45.

Do you want to get 'wonder-candles'?
Add a command that will, after the wind
finishes extinguishing them, make the candles
relight automatically. Make the wind keep on
trying to extinguish them.

Chapter 6

DESIGNING SHAPES

Advice: if you find this chapter difficult to understand jump the end for the summary. You should then be able to return and persevere with more success.

EXERCISE 1

☐Write a program that will print out the following pyramid.

The program should be designed in such a way that it will include only one PRINT AT command. It is worth you taking a few minutes to try and solve the problem by yourself and run your ideas on the computer.

_____

_____

_____

_____

_____

_____

? Having difficulty? Turn to the next page.

With the help of the following exercises you will be able to discover the secret of building the pyramid.

What does the following program do?

```
10 LET Y=9
12 LET A=6
14 LET B=14
20 FOR X=A TO B
30 PRINT AT Y,X;"█ "
40 NEXT X
```

After you have thought about it check it on the computer.

Now, are you able to write a program for the pyramid? (Try before you continue with Exercise 2.)

EXERCISE 2

If you have still not succeeded, here is a further exercise to help you. Change the program in Exercise 1 so that it will produce the line as before, plus another line like this:

The row from previous exercise
The additional row

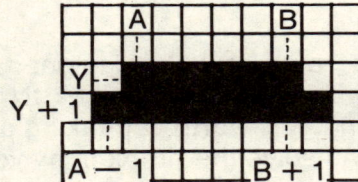

(Answer 46)

Now, having executed the 2 exercises successfully you should know how to write the pyramid program. If, in spite of this, you have still not succeeded look at Answer 47.

Let's 'play around' with the pyramid program!

A. Add commands to the program so that the computer will draw pyramids in different colours one after the other.

B. Add suitable commands to the program by using CHR$ so that when the computer draws the first pyramid, with CHR$ 33, it will return and draw over the previous one with CHR$34 and so on..... . (At the same time the colours should change.)

If you don't remember what CHR$ is turn to pages 34-35.

C. Change the program so that you will get the biggest possible pyramid.

D. What will happen if you swap the X and Y in the PRINT command?

PRINT AT X,Y; " □ "

Change it and check your theory.

E. What do you have to do to the program to produce this shape?

(Answer 48)

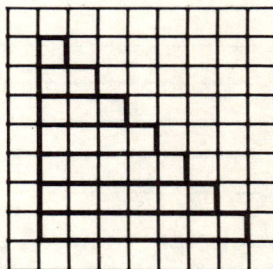

F. Are you interested in creating this shape? We'll leave you to work on it by yourself.......

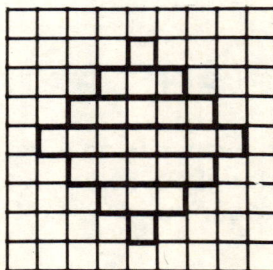

EXERCISE 3

Write a program that will draw rectangles one
after the other like this:

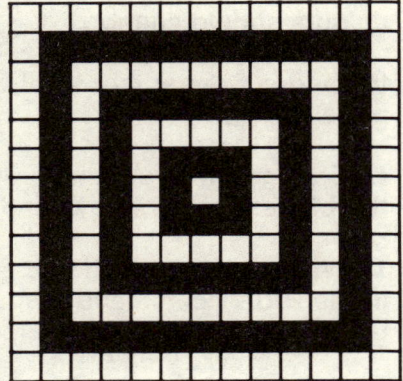

☐ Try to write the program on your own.

Hint: before the program can be written you
have to first work out how, in general, to draw a
rectangle. After that add the lines that will
duplicate and expand it. If you are having
difficulty turn to the exercise on the following
page.

HELPFUL EXERCISE

Now we'll design a program that will draw a
rectangle between columns A and B and
between rows C and D.

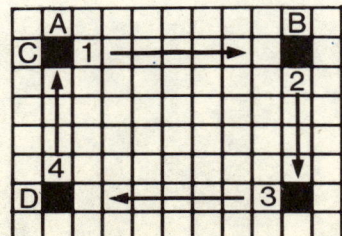

We will build the program in stages:

Stage A: write a program where the computer will draw side 1 from left to right (direction of arrow) Give A, B, and C any values you want. (Answer 49)

⬰ Run the program on the computer.

Stage B: add commands to the program which will get the computer to continue to draw side 2 from top to bottom: give D a value as well. (Answer 5Ø)

⬰ Run the program.

STAGE C: add suitable commands to the program that will draw side 3 (from right to left).

NOTE: you can use STEP–1.
(Answer 51)

⬰ Run the program on the computer.

STAGE D: it should not be too hard for you to complete the fourth side. Write the extra lines and run the program. This time we will not give you an answer. If you have problems drawing the fourth side go back and start the exercise from the beginning.

STAGE E: what has to happen to A, B, C?   (Answer 52)
Enter suitable commands, so that you will get 3 additional rectangles.

Again, play around with the program.

1. Add colours: get the computer to colour each rectangle in a different colour.
2. After the general program is finished, add another line that will make the computer draw the rectangles in the following way.

```
┌─────────────────────────┐
│    DRAWS RECTANGLES     │
└─────────────────────────┘

┌─────────────────────────┐
│       ERASES IT         │
└─────────────────────────┘

┌─────────────────────────┐
│  DRAWS A NEW BIGGER     │
│       RECTANGLE         │
└─────────────────────────┘
```

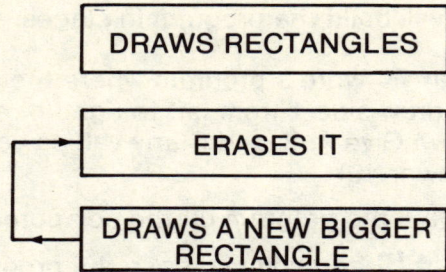

☐ Use CLS to erase the rectangle.

3. Add one command: after the large square is erased the program loops back and draws the small square and so on. After you have finished remove the CLS command.

4. Continue to play with the program:

● Change the size and position of the rectangles.

● Enter a change so that in each rectangle a different CHR$ will appear.

● Only change B and leave A, C and D the same. Run the program and see what you get.

YOU HAVE REACHED THE END OF THE SECOND UNIT

You have gone a considerable way. You already know how to write programs making extensive use of FOR–NEXT loops and variables. We saw in this unit that very varied graphics can be drawn using these commands. Perhaps, at this stage, you feel ready to let your imagination take flight. If so – no one can stop you....

A REVISION SESSION TO END WITH

Here is a list of concepts learned in this unit. Go over each and check whether you remember them. (You can refresh your memory by referring to the page numbers which appear in brackets beside them.)

(7) LET
(14) LET X=X+1
(11) VARIABLE
(13) BUG
(21) FOR–NEXT
(21) BREAK

(21) LOOP
(34) CHR$
(36) STEP
(38) NEGATIVE STEP
    COMPUTER MESSAGES
      2 (16)
      B (14)

Are you interested in a few difficult challenges?

Here are a number of suggestions for drawing shapes on the computer.

The programs are within your reach, but you will need patience to write them. If you are interested try them:

(Don't forget that your Spectrum+ has sound and colour...)

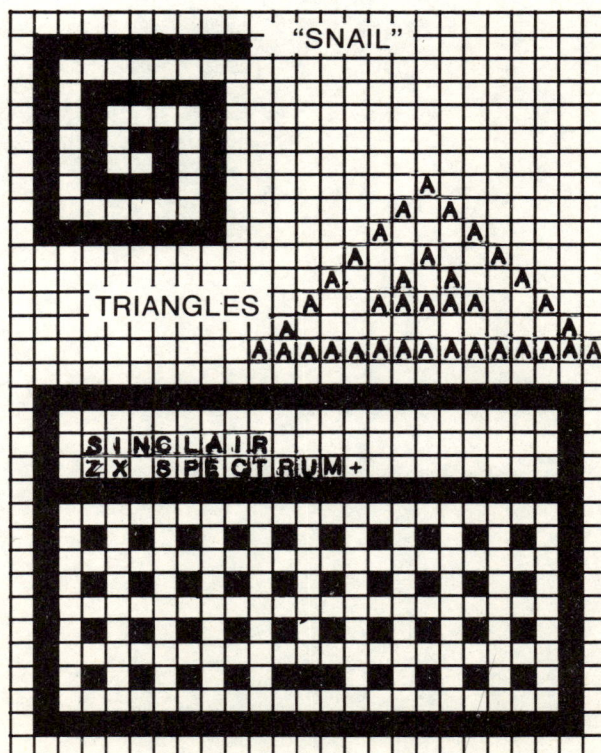

"SNAIL"

TRIANGLES

SINCLAIR
ZX SPECTRUM+

Answers

Answer 1

```
10 LET N=1 ---------------→ N=1
20 PRINT AT 10,15;"N";N ---→N=1   N=2   N=3   N=4
25 PAUSE 20              ┌----→N=2   N=3   N=4
• 30 LET N=N+1 ----------┘  ┌--→N=2   N=3   N=4
40 GO TO 20 ---------------┘
```

• *N increased by 1 in this line*

Answer 2

```
10 LET N=2
20 PRINT AT 10,15;N
25 PAUSE 20
30 LET N=N+2    ........ This is the amended command
40 GO TO 20
```

Answer 3

```
10 LET M=0
20 PRINT M;    ........... Semi colon continues to print in the
```
same line.
```
30 LET M=M+1
40 GO TO 20        Go back to 20 and not to 10
```

Answer 4

```
10 LET M=0
20 PRINT M;",";    ........... It is important to use the semi-
```
colon, so that the computer will print in the same line.
```
30 LET M=M+1
40 GO TO 20
```

Answer 5

The additional line is:

```
25 BEEP 0,2,10
```

Answer 6

```
25 BEEP Ø,2,M
```

Answer 7

```
30 LET M=M+1
```

Answer 8

```
1Ø LET Y=1
2Ø PRINT AT Y,11;"A"
3Ø LET Y=Y+3        jump down 3 lines
4Ø GO TO 2Ø       in column 11
```

Answer 9

Line 2Ø changes to:

```
2Ø PRINT AT Y,11;Y
```

Prints the value of the variable Y.

Answer 1Ø

```
 5 LET N=Ø
1Ø LET Y=1
2Ø PRINT INK N; AT Y,11;" ■"
3Ø LET Y=Y+3
35 LET N=N+1
4Ø GO TO 2Ø
```

Answer 11

```
25 BEEP Ø.2,N*3
```

Answer 12

The PAUSE in line 3Ø increases! In the first cycle X=1 and so PAUSE X*X=1. In the second cycle X=2 and so PAUSE X*X=4 and so on. The PAUSE increases and the program 'gets tired'.

Answer 13

and thus you get a diagonal

Let's look at the line:

```
20 PRINT AT M,M,"█ "
```

When M increases by 1 (in line 30), the number of the row increases by 1 and so does the number of the column:

Answer 14

```
                              RUN
10 FOR N=1 TO 3 .........  N=1  N=2  N=3
20 PRINT AT 10,15;N ......  N=1   N=2   N=3
30 NEXT N ...............  N=2   N=3   N=4
40 PRINT "END" ..........  END
```

When N becomes larger than 3 (TO 3) the computer leaves the FOR...NEXT loop and goes to line 40.

Answer 15

```
10 FOR N=0 TO 7
20 BORDER N
30 BEEP 0.2,N
40 NEXT N
50 GO TO 10
```

Answer 16

```
25 PAPER 7-N: CLS
```

When N=0, PAPER=7 and when N=7, PAPER=0. CLS colours the whole screen in the PAPER colour.

Answer 17

```
10 FOR N=14 TO 16
15 BEEP 0.1,Y*3
20 PRINT AT N,N;"A"
30 NEXT N
```

Answer 18

You should have added:

```
40 LET X=16
50 FOR Y=10 TO 16
55 BEEP 0.1
60 PRINT AT Y,X;"A"
70 LET X=X-1
80 NEXT Y
```

Answer 19

```
 5 LET X=8
10 FOR Y=6 TO 10
20 PRINT INK Y-4; AT Y,X;"MARY"
25 BEEP 0.2,Y*4
30 LET X=X+2
40 NEXT Y
```

Answer 20

```
10 FOR S=0 TO 59
20 PRINT AT 10,15;S
25 PAUSE 25
30 NEXT S          S – seconds
```

Answer 21

The line added is:
```
40 GO TO 10
```

Answer 22

When the computer goes back and begins to count from 0, the figure 9 remains from the previous cycle.

Answer 23

```
35 PRINT AT 10,15,"⬜⬜"  (⬜= SPACE)
```

Answer 24

```
25 PAUSE 49
```

Answer 25

Print Colon	`2 PRINT AT 10,14;":"`
Minutes Loop	`4 FOR M=0 TO 59`
Print Minutes	`6 PRINT AT 10,12;M`
Seconds Loop	`10 FOR S=0 TO 59`
Print Seconds	`20 PRINT AT 10,15;S`
	`25 PAUSE 48`
End of Seconds Loop	`30 NEXT S`
Erase Seconds	`35 PRINT AT 10,15;"▢▢"`
End of Minutes Loop	`36 NEXT M`
Erase Minutes Loop	`38 PRINT AT 10,12;"▢▢"`
Return to start	`40 GO TO 4`

Answer 26

The answer is NO! You cannot have crossing loops in a program.

Answer 27

We added the following lines to the clock program:

```
21 FOR N=3 TO 26
22 PRINT INK N/6; AT 4,N;"██
23 NEXT N:PAUSE 2
24 FOR N=3 TO 26
25 PRINT AT 4,N;"▢▢"
26 NEXT N: BEEP 0,2,10
```

Answer 28

```
10 FOR X=5 TO 15
20 PRINT AT 4,X;"+"
30 NEXT Y
```

Answer 29

```
10 FOR Y=3 TO 15
20 PRINT AT Y,4;"+"
30 NEXT Y
```

Answer 30

```
10 FOR Y=3 TO 7
20 FOR X=5 TO 13
30 PRINT AT Y,X;"+"
40 NEXT X
50 NEXT Y
```

Answer 31

```
10 FOR X=2 TO 5
20 FOR Y=2 TO 5
30 PRINT AT Y,X;" "
40 NEXT Y
50 NEXT X
```

Answer 32

The change is:

```
 5 LET A=0
10 FOR X=2+A TO 5+A
20 FOR Y=2+A TO 5+A
```

Every change of A will print the square in a different place along the diagonal on the screen.

Answer 33

You should add:

```
60 LET A=A+3
70 GO TO 10
```

Answer 34

```
30 PRINT INK A/3; AT Y,X;"█"
```

Answer 35

```
55 BEEP 0.2,A
```

Answer 36

Begin in column 2	`10 LET X=2`
Carry out the loop 5 times	`20 FOR N=1 TO 5`
Print in column X	`30 PRINT AT 4,X;"$"`
Jump 4 columns	`40 LET X=X+4`
End of the loop	`50 NEXT N`

Answer 37

```
10 FOR Y=2 TO 8 STEP 3
20 FOR X=2 TO 18 STEP 4
30 PRINT AT 4,X;"$"
40 NEXT X
50 NEXT Y
```

This is the old loop

This is the additional loop which causes the old loop to be performed in 3 lines on the screen!

Answer 38

```
10 LET Y=0
20 FOR X=21 TO 0 STEP -1
30 PRINT INK X/3; AT Y, X;"█"
40 LET Y=Y+1
50 NEXT X
```

Answer 39

```
40 PRINT AT Y+1, X-1;"████"
```

one line below one column left

Answer 40

```
5Ø PRINT AT X+2,X-1;"█ █"
```

Answer 41

The line 2Ø LET X=2 changes to 2Ø FOR X=2 TO 17 STEP 5 and at the end, line 6Ø NEXT X is added.

Answer 42

```
1Ø FOR Y=1 TO 11 STEP 5
2Ø FOR X=2 TO 17 STEP 5
3Ø PRINT AT Y,X;CHR$ 34
4Ø PRINT AT Y+1,X-1;"███ █"
5Ø PRINT AT Y+2,X-1;"█ █"
6Ø NEXT Y
7Ø NEXT Y
```

Draw one robot | Draw a line of robots | Draw 3 lines of robots

Answer 43

```
1Ø FOR X=5 TO 25
2Ø PRINT AT 4,X;">"
25 PAUSE 5
3Ø PRINT AT 4,X;"□ "
4Ø NEXT X
5Ø GO TO 1Ø
```

Answer 44

```
  3 FOR N=1 TO 6
  5 PRINT INK N; AT 4,4;"█"; AT 4,26;"█"
 1Ø FOR X=5 TO 25
 2Ø PRINT AT 4,X;">"
 25 BEEP Ø.1,X
 3Ø PRINT AT 4,X;"□ "
 4Ø NEXT X
 5Ø FOR X=25 TO 5 STEP -1
 6Ø PRINT AT 4,X;"<"
 7Ø BEEP Ø.1,X
 8Ø PRINT AT 4,X;"□ "
 9Ø NEXT X
1ØØ NEXT N
```

Answer 45

Picture of 4 lighted candlesticks

```
10 FOR X=10 TO 25 STEP 5
20 PRINT INK 2; AT 9,X;"*"; INK 4; AT 10,X;"█"; AT 11,X;"█";
   INK 5; AT 12,X-1;"████████"
30 NEXT X
40 FOR X=0 TO 31
50 PRINT AT 9,X;">"
55 PAUSE 5
60 PRINT AT 9,X;"□"
70 NEXT X
```

The wind moves right.

Answer 46

The following lines are added:

```
16 FOR Y=9 TO 10
50 LET A=A-1
60 LET B=B+1
70 NEXT Y
```

Answer 47

```
10 LET A=15: LET B=15
15 FOR Y=3 TO 18
20 FOR X=A TO B
25 BEEP 0.03,Y
30 PRINT INK Y/3; AT Y,X;"█"
40 NEXT X
50 LET A=A-1 : LET B=B+1
60 NEXT Y
```

Answer 48

You should erase LET A=A-1 in line 50.

Answer 49

```
1Ø LET A=13: LET B=16: LET C=9
2Ø FOR X=A TO B
3Ø PRINT AT C,X;"█"
4Ø NEXT X
```

Answer 50

```
12 LET D=13
6Ø FOR C=C TO D
7Ø PRINT AT Y,B;"█"
8Ø NEXT Y
```

Answer 51

```
 9Ø FOR X=B TO A STEP -1
1ØØ PRINT AT D,X;"█"
11Ø NEXT X
```

Answer 52

You should add:

```
 15 FOR N=1 TO 4
15Ø LET A=A-2 : LET B=B+2 : LET C=C-2 : LET D=D+2
16Ø NEXT N
```

SOLUTION TO THE "SNAIL"

Inner section of the snail

```
10 LET A=15
20 LET B=1
30 LET C=10
40 FOR X=A TO A+B
45 PRINT AT C,X;"■
48 NEXT X
50 FOR Y=C TO C+B+1
55 PRINT AT Y,A+B;"■ "
58 NEXT Y
60 FOR X=A+B TO A-2 STEP -1
65 PRINT AT C+B+1,X;" ■
68 NEXT X
70 FOR Y=C+B+1 TO C-2 STEP -1
75 PRINT AT Y,A-2;" ■ "
78 NEXT Y
```

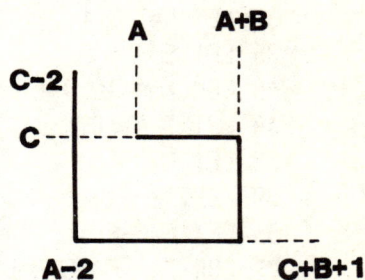

Next section of the snail

```
100 LET A=A-Z
110 LET C=C-2
120 LET B=B+4
130 GO TO 40
```

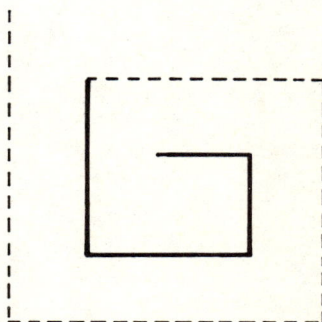

SOLUTION TO THE TRIANGLES:

```
10 LET A=15
20 LET C=8
30 LET D=11
35 LET E=3
40 FOR X=A TO A+E
50 PRINT AT C,X
55 LET C=C+1
60 NEXT X
65 LET C=C-E
70 FOR X=A+E TO A-E STEP 1
80 PRINT AT D,X;"A"
90 NEXT X
100 FOR X=A-E TO A
110 PRINT AT D,X;"A"
120 LET D=D-1
130 NEXT X
132 LET D=D+E
135 LET C=C-3
140 LET D=D+3
150 LET E=E+4
160 GO TO 40
```

Draws side one

Restores C

Draws side two

Draws side three

Restores D

Increase for next

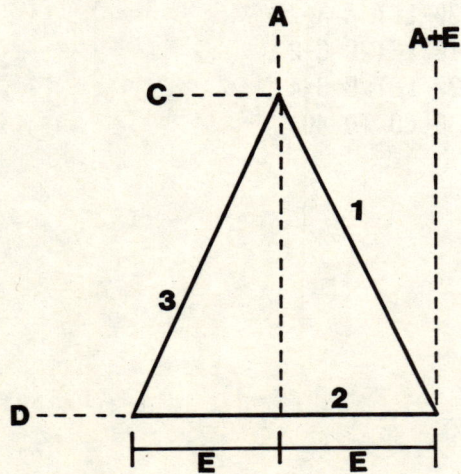

SOLUTION TO SPECTRUM+

```
 10 LET L=3
 20 FOR Y=1 TO 2
 30 FOR X=5 TO 25
 40 PRINT AT L,X;"▄▄"
 50 NEXT X
 60 LET L=15
 70 NEXT Y
 80 LET L=4
 90 FOR X=1 TO 2
100 FOR Y=3 TO 14
110 PRINT AT Y,L;" ▮"
120 NEXT Y
130 PRINT AT 3,25;"▜"
140 PRINT AT 15,4;" ▪"
150 LET L=25
160 NEXT X
170 FOR X=5 TO 24
180 PRINT AT 7,X;"▀"
190 NEXT X
200 PRINT AT 7,25;"▜"
210 FOR X=5 TO 23 STEP 2
220 PRINT AT 8,X;"▀"
230 PRINT AT 10,X;"▀"
240 PRINT AT 12,X;"▀"
250 PRINT AT 14,X;"▀"
260 NEXT X
270 PRINT AT 14,14;"▀"
280 INK 3
290 PRINT AT 4,5;"SINCLAIR"
300 PRINT AT 5,5;"ZX Spectrum+"
```

This loop draws the case

This loop draws the keys

NOTES